Robert Orchardson
Endless façade

Foreword

It is particularly satisfying that this exhibition is shared by Ikon and the Contemporary Art Gallery, marking a point of personal as well as institutional significance. It signals a new partnership for each organisation, one that extends from a mutual interest in each other's programmes, ethos and underlining philosophy, as well as our similar origins. Both galleries were founded by artists and although now very different as shifts have occurred over time, it is a legacy and spirit that we constantly reflect on and hold dear.

In this vein British artist Robert Orchardson's work could not be more apposite. His artistic proposition compels us to reassess utopias of the past, this revisiting however more than a mere act of longing. Instead it implies a restaging of unfulfilled possibilities as he grapples with fresh meaning and opportunity.

Orchardson makes sculptures inspired by science fiction and futuristic design. Using low-tech materials — wood, resin, aluminium — he is unashamedly nostalgic for modernist idealism, appropriating its forms and reconfiguring these as objects devoid of apparent function. Orchardson considers prototypes and models to be carriers for ideas, able to convey utopian potential as they develop into something beyond themselves. He also sees this sense of possibility inherent in stage sets, where a narrative exists between the material character of the set itself, and the 'other' identity it adopts within the context of a play.

Endless façade is an ambitious new installation which partially revisits stage sets designed by Isamu Noguchi in 1955 for a Royal Shakespeare Company production of *King Lear*. Noguchi aspired to an other-worldly feeling, where abstract, mobile forms created a shifting landscape against which the play unfolded. However his designs were met with damning criticism, regarded as outlandish and unsympathetic to the theatrical production. Fascinated by aspiration offset by failure Orchardson has revisited Noguchi's designs, grasping their optimism and eventual redundancy, transforming the galleries into an immersive environment tense with possibility. Huge monochrome wall constructions, brightly coloured geometric objects, screens made of complex triangular forms, light and shadow, all play their part in mediating our understanding of the spaces and our view of other visitors. They create a new 'stage' in which viewers assume the position of actors. For Orchardson such machinations are key.

We are indebted to the individuals and organisations that have supported this, the first solo museum exhibition for Orchardson with presentations in the UK and Canada. Amanda and Anthony Wilkinson at Wilkinson Gallery, London and Ben Kaufmann of Galerie Ben Kaufmann, Berlin, along with their respective staff have been most helpful in propelling this exhibition onward. Thanks too go to the Kirkland Collection, London for the loan of the earlier work *Perfect Vacuum* thus enriching the dialogue with Orchardson's practice through its presentation as part of *Endless façade*. Matthew Rampley has contributed an insightful essay, crucial as a new in-depth piece of writing on Orchardson's work. As such it plays a major part in this publication, the first to evaluate his practice as a whole.

Above all we thank Robert Orchardson. Through his quiet intelligence, curiosity, attention to detail, and importantly his optimism in seeking out the potential in that seemingly now forgotten, we view things afresh.

Nigel Prince, Director, Contemporary Art Gallery
Jonathan Watkins, Director, Ikon Gallery

In Search of Futures Past

Robert Orchardson's work testifies to the enduring fascination of the avant-garde utopias of the 1910s and the 1920s, in particular, Soviet Constructivism, even as they recede ever more into the past and beyond living memory. Revisiting the aesthetic language of a futuristic modernism that characterised not only certain kinds of artistic practice but also much popular culture of the twentieth century, his work is a response to the question: what is the meaning of such forms in the wake of the 'decline of modernism' and the optimism that produced them?[1] In other words, given that the avant-garde has now 'aged,' its products now objects in historical displays in museums and galleries, can we relate to them in terms other than those of nostalgia and remembrance?

Orchardson is not the first artist to have broached this topic. When the Minimalist sculptors Robert Morris, Carl Andre and Donald Judd began exhibiting featureless geometric objects in the 1960s — flat sheets of lead, zinc or copper laid on the gallery floor, or rectangular boxes installed lengthways on the floor or in vertical columns on the wall — they were reprising a central theme of the work of Constructivist sculptor Vladimir Tatlin, namely, emphasis on materiality in space in order to undermine the idealist aesthetics of pre-revolutionary bourgeois culture. Devoid of intrinsic aesthetic interest — they were made from commonly available industrial materials — Minimalist sculptures compelled the viewer to attend to their material composition and structure and thereby reflect on his / her own physical relation to the objects and the gallery space where they were displayed. More recently, since the 1990s, Liam Gillick has used the primary geometric structures, forms and colours of Piet Mondrian or the Dutch designer Gerrit Rietveld in his sculptural investigation of spaces of social interaction which, while maintaining critical distance from the concept of 'utopia,' examine the place of art in a post-utopian era.[2]

The work of Orchardson sits within this lineage, rearticulating the lexicon of visual forms that functioned within avant-garde art and design as signifiers of a utopian desire systematically to alter the world. As such, Orchardson, who has also talked of his interest in the work of the Soviet architect Konstantin Melnikov or of Bruno Taut, one of the leading designers of modernist social housing in the Weimar Republic, undertakes an archaeology of utopias of the twentieth century. This is visibly the case in *Melnikov* (2007), a mixed-media installation that includes a screen with a honey-comb lattice structure — its shadow then projected onto the wall behind — that quotes from Melnikov's best known building, the tower of the house in Moscow he designed for himself in the late 1920s. Melnikov was a major architect but fell out of favour with the Stalinist espousal of Neo-Classicism. Hence, as Orchardson has himself noted, "it is a sad but interesting irony that he became something of a reclusive hermit living in what had once been a vision of new, ambitious future, his modernist tower both a symbol of potential and testament to failed ambition."[3]

The archaeology of utopia can be found in other works too, such as Orchardson's *Aelita* (2007), a spray-painted steel corner-mounted geometric framework sculpture that evokes the corner reliefs of Tatlin. The title gives other meanings to this piece, for *Aelita* was also one of the first full-length science-fiction films, made in the Soviet Union in 1924 by Yakov Protozanov, with futuristic stage sets and costumes by the constructivist designer Alexandra Exter. Orchardson's *Aelita* also recalls the spatial constructions of Tatlin's contemporaries Naum Gabo and Alexander Rodchenko, whose faith in the utopian capacities of technology to effect social transformation inspired works that appeared to be the prototypes for unspecified engineering structures. Other sculptures by Orchardson return to this utopian practice in which the distinction between art and engineering design was briefly put into question; these include *Sequoia Transfer* (2004) an acrylic spiral painted on a circular wooden surface that evokes Rodchenko's *Spatial Construction No. 12*

Aelita (2007)
United Kingdom Government Art Collection

Melnikov (2007)
Fondazione Sandretto Re Rebaudengo

(1920–1921), or *Symmetriad* (2004), a hanging wooden crystalline structure and *Terminal Velocity* (2005), a large-scale free-standing frame housing what looks like the schematic diagram of a geometric structure, pulled apart by a vortex in the centre of the frame.

Both *Symmetriad* and *Terminal Velocity* recall the convergence of art and technology in the avant-garde, although here the three-dimensional model has been flattened into a two-dimensional sculptural drawing. The immediate source for *Symmetriad* was Stanley Kubrick's *2001: A Space Odyssey* of 1968; slowing down the animated stargate sequence from the end of the film, Orchardson remade it as a static structure. This freezing of an ephemeral image played off its immateriality against the abstracted form of the sculpture. The title of *Symmetriad* is also relevant here. Taken from the 1961 science fiction novel *Solaris* by Stanisław Lem, it denoted the constantly changing strange amorphous forms on the surface of the planet. At first utterly alien, for a few moments they would then take the form of a recognisable shape; an object or figure familiar to the viewer, before shifting back to becoming an abstract mass. As Orchardson has said, "I am interested in making sculptures that do something of this — perhaps appearing entirely abstract, but then there are moments of familiarity, or times when a sculpture implies some sort of function. As such the works become more interesting and hard to pin down."[4]

Amongst his more recent works, *The Future is Certain, Give Us Time to Work it Out* (2009), a sequence of fourteen upright triangular aluminium panels, continues this engagement. Alongside its title, richly suggestive of the naive utopian confidence of the interwar period (one is reminded of the unalloyed optimism of the 1940 General Motors film *Towards New Horizons*) *The Future is Certain…* also foregrounds the fetishism of certain forms and materials, in particular, chrome, steel and aluminium, all three aesthetically seductive signifiers of the triumphantly progressive industrial modernity of the twentieth century.

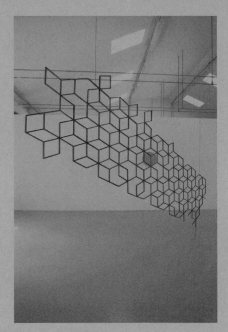

Symmetriad (2004)

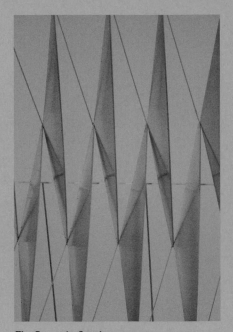

The Future is Certain,
Give Us Time to Work it Out (2009)

Orchardson works with a vocabulary of forms — the diagonal line, crystalline structures, and obliquely intersecting masses, acutely attenuated rhomboids — that came to connote the aspirations of progressive avant-garde designers, artists and architects. Signifiers of dynamic speed and of the spatial and temporal reorientation of modern technology, they functioned as metonymic representatives of a futuristic design that could be found in diverse works such as the typographic designs of Jan Tschichold, the advertising imagery of Edward McKnight Kauffer or the Vorticist paintings of Wyndham Lewis. *The Future is Certain...* employs this geometry of futurity, but the largest-scale work in this vein is *Nexus* (2007), an epoxy-coated nine-metre tall steel dart-like projectile that looks as if it has just fallen to earth, stabbing the pavement in front of the headquarters of British Land plc in Seymour Street in London.

Other pieces, such as *Black Air* (2005) or *Interstellar* (2006) arrange the same futuristic rhomboids as floor pieces, a gesture towards the horizontal schemas of Minimalism, although, with its insistent forward motion and aerodynamic form, *Black Air* could easily pass for an example of contemporary aeronautic design, the prototype, perhaps, of the latest generation of stealth aircraft. A third piece, exhibited as *The Substance of Things Unseen* in the plaza of the Economist Building in London in 2005, arranges these same elements in a spiral circulating around a void in the centre, like some gigantic camera aperture. In fact, the sculpture (entitled *Carousel* in contrast to the installation in the Economist Building) is based on the crystal 'carousel' of the 1976 science fiction film *Logan's Run*, which vaporises all citizens of an 'idyllic' city on reaching 30. It also plays off against its location — a building by Alison and Peter Smithson, two of the leading modernist architects of postwar Britain. The presence of this evocation of a dystopic future at the headquarters of *The Economist* magazine, one of the most upbeat neo-liberal advocates of the virtues of the capitalist economy, creates a jarring juxtaposition which, since the banking crisis of 2008, has taken on a new resonance.

Carousel (2005)

Nexus (2007)
Collection British Land PLC

Orchardson thus achieved, with a configuration of minimal geometric elements, a richly suggestive installation, and to those meanings already intimated can be added the significance of its title and the allusions of the sculpture to the crown of thorns at the summit of Oskar Niemeyer's Metropolitan Cathedral of Brasilia. The title is a truncated biblical quotation; the original, from the *Book of Hebrews* (11.1), reads "Now faith is the substance of things hoped for, the evidence of things not seen." This explicitly religious formula may seem incongruent in this context, but that is the point. Both the avant-garde faith in the future and the neo-liberalism of *The Economist* are, Orchardson's work suggests, types of secular theology.

The popular cultural references of *Carousel* and *Symmetriad* recur in other works, too. *Rheya* (2006), two painted plywood propeller constructions suspended from the ceiling (incidentally reminiscent of the mobiles of Alexander Calder), is named after the deceased wife of Kris Kelvin, the principle protagonist of *Solaris*. Although dead, she reappears in the space station orbiting the planet Solaris, an apparition created by the planet itself; the simulation of Rheya (Hari in Lem's original Polish) exists in a suspended state between irreality (Rheya is, after all, dead, and Kelvin realises he is facing a psychological construct) and reality (it does not realise it is not Rheya and seems indestructible). In *Kelvin* (2007) Orchardson reuses the propeller form but this time installs it on the floor, propping it up against the wall. This interest in science fiction and popular culture is evident elsewhere, too. *World without Walls* (2005) also references *2001: A Space Odyssey* while *Integral Model* (2005) is inspired by the dystopian science-fiction novel *We* (1927) by the Russian émigré writer Yevgeny Zamyatin.

For avant-garde artists the rhomboid, of which Orchardson makes frequent use, represented the transformation of the static rectangle into a visual symbol of the pulse of a machine-made culture of speed. However, the critical connotations of *The Substance of Things Unseen* also summon up the dystopic

World without Walls (2005)
Saatchi Collection

Kelvin (2007)

potentials of its oblique geometries in which, as in the set design for Robert Wiene's 1920 film *The Cabinet of Dr. Caligari*, they signify expressionist paranoia, or create the oppressive atmosphere of Fritz Lang's futuristic *Metropolis* (1927) or Isamu Noguchi's 1955 stage set for *King Lear* — a futuristic version of the play which was criticised for the outlandish design. However, in its diamond form the rhomboid possesses a double meaning as crystal, symbol of the convergence of the organic and mineralogical, biology and geology.

The crystal had already been espoused as a symbol of life within the inert processes of mineral growth by the Romantics, and in the twentieth century it again reappeared as a powerful artistic and cultural motif. For the crystal came to symbolise "the purification of 'raw life' and its transformation into beauty;" in which the "social meaning of modern building, seen as the origin of aesthetic form, is nothing other than the 'inner geometry' of nature, now filled with life."[5] In 1914 the painter Wenzel Hablik imagined a crystal castle floating in the sea, while Hans Scharoun, a leading expressionist architect, depicted the modern city as a crystal plant shooting upwards from its mineral roots. Bruno Taut's book *Alpine Architecture*, published in 1917, put forward the notion of a chain of crystalline architectural structures spanning the Alps (never built, of course), while in his earlier book, *The City Crown* (1915), Taut envisaged a city with a fantastic crystalline building at its centre; "Flooded by the light of the sun, the crystal house reigns over everything like a flashing diamond, sparkling in the sun as a symbol of the highest serenity, joyfulness and spiritual delight."[6]

The crystal symbolised the utopian dream of a new religion that would overcome human alienation from nature, and Taut's ideas are taken up in Orchardson's *Alpine Architecture* (2008). The installation employs a larger version of the aluminium structure seen in *The Future is Certain…*, but here accompanied by wooden benches (an allusion to Donald Judd's turn to furniture in his later career, perhaps). Companion pieces to *Alpine Architecture* include a sequence of images printed onto pages of National Geographic magazines, such as *Chapel* (2008) in which the viewer is faced with a triangular glass corridor, a passageway in some high-tech structure that also evokes the expressionist cathedrals that reworked the language of Gothic architecture.

Orchardson's oeuvre to date thus represents a sustained investigation of the formal legacy of utopian imaginaries, both in avant-garde architecture and design and also in popular culture. But what are the stakes of this restaging? At first sight it might seem that his translation of these utopian constructions into a post-minimalist sculptural language constitutes a kind of betrayal, in which the avant-garde project of sublating art and life is overturned and placed back into the familiar context of the art gallery.[7] Supporting this contention might be the fact that his works also exercise a seductive appeal; the sheen of the smooth gloss surfaces of *Black Air* or *Nexus*, for example, the rhythmic regularity of *Alpine Architecture* or *The Substance of Things Unseen*, or the precarious flimsiness of the screens of *Melnikov* and *Symmetriad* generate a distinctive aesthetic, a poetic sequence of forms that seemingly stands at odds with their borrowed visions of an engineered technological future. In this respect both *Symmetriad* and *Terminal Velocity* offer a kind of artistic rebuke to the faith in instrumental rationality; instead of a neatly organised array of cubic forms they present the viewer with a manic and hypertrophic jumble. Reminiscent of Sol LeWitt's serial sculptures, they present a decentered autopoietic (and crystalline) rationality which, as Rosalind Krauss has suggested in relation to LeWitt, can be seen as articulating a critique of the relentless growth of the instrumental reason of modernity.[8]

Observers have noted the strange conflict between the formal syntax of Orchardson's work, which connotes the high-tech dreams of avant-garde utopias, and the materials he uses. For although the pieces executed in

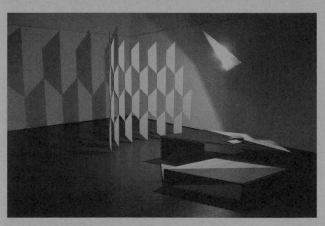

Melnikov (2007)
Fondazione Sandretto Re Rebaudengo

Chapel (2008)
Private Collection

aluminium or steel imply a congruence of matter and form, others are made of MDF, plywood or found objects and materials that are often broken or discarded, robbed of their original function. There is an opposition between the two, in which elevated ambitions are encountered with the most banal of materials. Yet this is no deflationary tactic aimed at the grandiose vision of the architects and designers of the early twentieth century; rather, it points to the complexities of utopianism itself. First, it should be noted that Orchardson's use of wood consciously echoes the practices of Soviet Constructivism; for all their commitment to new technologies, many of the constructions of Tatlin, Gabo and Rodchenko were, in fact, made of nothing more substantial than cardboard or wood. Tatlin's most famous project, the *Monument to the Third International* (1919), which was intended to be a steel and glass structure higher than the Eiffel Tower, never reached beyond the status of a large-scale wooden maquette; likewise the iron surfaces of Gabo's engineered *Heads* should be placed alongside his cardboard and wooden *Torsos*.

The contradiction between the execution of these maquettes and the original vision was in part a reflection of the exigencies of the time; lack of materials compelled a reliance on substitutes. However, it can also prompt us into reflection on the origins and nature of utopian thinking. In this context it is worth invoking the writings of one of the most important writers on utopia in the twentieth century, Ernst Bloch (1885–1977). Bloch is best known as the author of *The Spirit of Utopia* (1917) and *The Principle of Hope* (1938–1947), but what is not often analysed is his critical commentary on utopianism in the visual arts. For Bloch modernism "claimed to be a purging of the mustiness of the previous century and its unspeakable decoration. But the longer it went on … the more clearly the motto emerges as an inscription over the Bauhaus and that which is connected with it: Hurrah, we've run out of ideas."[9] He was also fiercely critical of "that part of the art of engineering which claims to be so progressive and which so rapidly stagnates, so rapidly ends up on the

Black Air (2007)

scrap-heap."[10] The utopia of transparency resulted, for Bloch, in the "kitsch of light" or in "chromium-plated misery." A fundamental weakness of modern architecture was the fact that "in its greatest transparency it reveals no content."[11]

What lay behind this criticism? At its heart was a concern with the roots of utopian thinking. In a passage from *The Spirit of Utopia* entitled 'On the Metaphysics of our Darkness' Bloch emphasised the self-intransparency of the human subject to itself. The self is a dark shadow, he claimed, a point of blindness to itself. There is no interior monologue of intimate self-knowledge, only self-alienation. "I cannot even experience and occupy myself ... only immediately afterward can I easily hold [my self], turn it before, me, so to speak."[12] And later: "only just after it passes can what was experienced be held up in front of oneself ... half still just experientially real and half already a juxtaposition of inactive contents."[13] The self is always trying to catch up with the deferred meanings of its experiences which, at the point of the now, remain a point of dark indeterminacy. Yet it is precisely the process of overcoming this lack, Bloch argued, that lies behind the utopian impulse. The blind spot of the self is thus a *productive* lacuna, giving rise to an anticipatory consciousness that operates in the gap between the (undetermined) present and projected future meanings.

The point of Bloch's critique was that certain kinds of utopian ideals in architecture and design aimed to entirely remove this constitutive indeterminacy in a kind of aesthetic hygiene (he identified 'lavatoriality' as the predominant feature of this avant-garde practice); the consequence of this was a semantic impoverishment, a production of empty forms. Anticipatory consciousness, in contrast, inhabits a world of semantic surplus that is always trying to supply the present with new significance. The meaning of each moment never fully decided, and looking at the past (Bloch's *The Principle of Hope* is a quasi historical encyclopaedia of utopianism, ranging from daydreams, fairytales, clothing, architecture, theatre, art, technology, music and religion) thus involves returning to what might have been. Historical retrieval is thus not an archaeological unearthing of dead relics of the past, but rather a revisiting of possible futures.

Arguably, the contradictions in Orchardson's work between form and material, their multiple references to utopias of the past in both popular culture and the high modernism of the avant-garde, and their staging of encounters between utopian and dystopian visions, function in precisely the same productive fashion outlined by Bloch. As Orchardson has noted, "I don't want to simply quote moments. I'm more interested in what they seem to do, and how they resonate as a whole, how they might help to articulate a broader sensibility ..." In other words, for all its rich depth of historical allusions, this is not a merely academic or nostalgic immersion in the past, but an exploration of the possibilities of reinvented meanings.

The idea of deferred meaning has enjoyed considerable currency; Sigmund Freud analysed it in relation to the concept of supplementarity ('Nachträglichkeit') while Jacques Derrida's notion of 'différance' likewise highlighted the chain of substitutions and the metonymic sliding of signifiers that eluded final semantic resolution. It was by mobilising these ideas that the American critic Hal Foster interpreted modernism as "a complex relay of anticipated futures and reconstructed pasts ..."[14] In the light of Bloch the specific role of utopian consciousness within the process becomes a little clearer. Returning to the initial question as to how to respond to the 'decline' of modernism, Orchardson's work compels, perhaps, a reassessment of the initial premises of the question; while we no longer hold to the artistic utopias of the past, the futurity of their horizons means that revisiting them is no simple act of nostalgia, but rather a restaging of new unfulfilled possibilities.

Matthew Rampley

1   Peter Bürger, *The Decline of Modernism* (Philadelphia, 1992).

2   See Liam Gillick, 'For a Functional Utopia,' *Utopia Station* (Venice, 2003).

3   Robert Orchardson in correspondence with the author, 15 January 2011.

4   Ibid.

5   Regine Prange, 'The Crystalline' in Keith Hartley, ed., *The Romantic Spirit in German Art 1790–1990* (London and Edinburgh, 1994) p. 159.

6   Bruno Taut, *The City Crown*, cited in Iain Boyd Whyte, 'Introduction' to Whyte, ed., *Modernism and the Spirit of the City* (London, 2003) p. 17.

7   On this definition of the avant-garde see Peter Bürger, *Theory of the Avant-Garde* (Manchester, 1986).

8   Rosalind Krauss, 'LeWitt in Progress,' in *The Originality of the Avantgarde and other Modernist Myths* (Cambridge, MA, 1985) pp. 244–259.

9   *PH*, II, p. 735.

10   Ibid.

11   *PH*, II, p. 736.

12   *SU*, p. 187.

13   *SU*, p. 199.

14   Hal Foster, *The Return of the Real* (Cambridge, MA, 1996) p. 29.

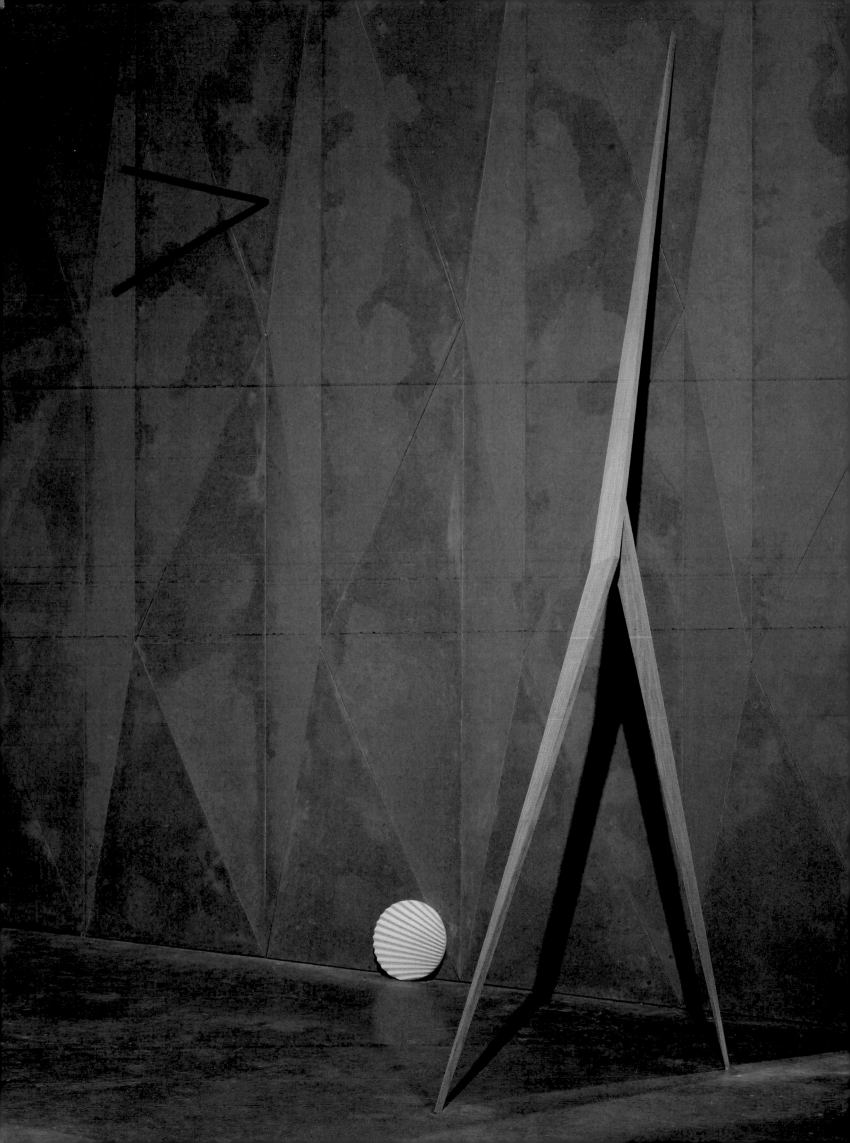

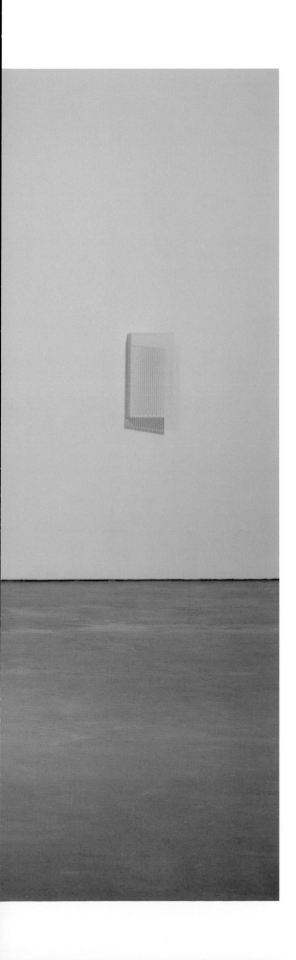

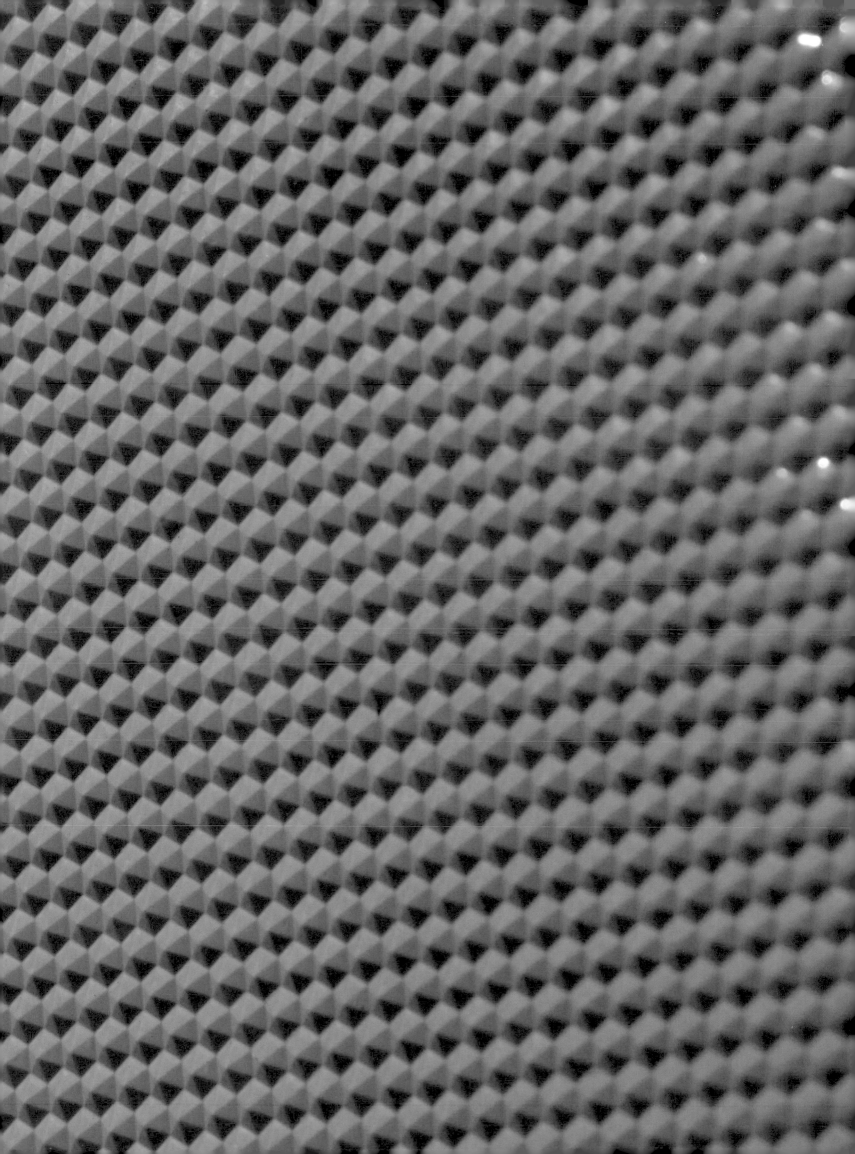

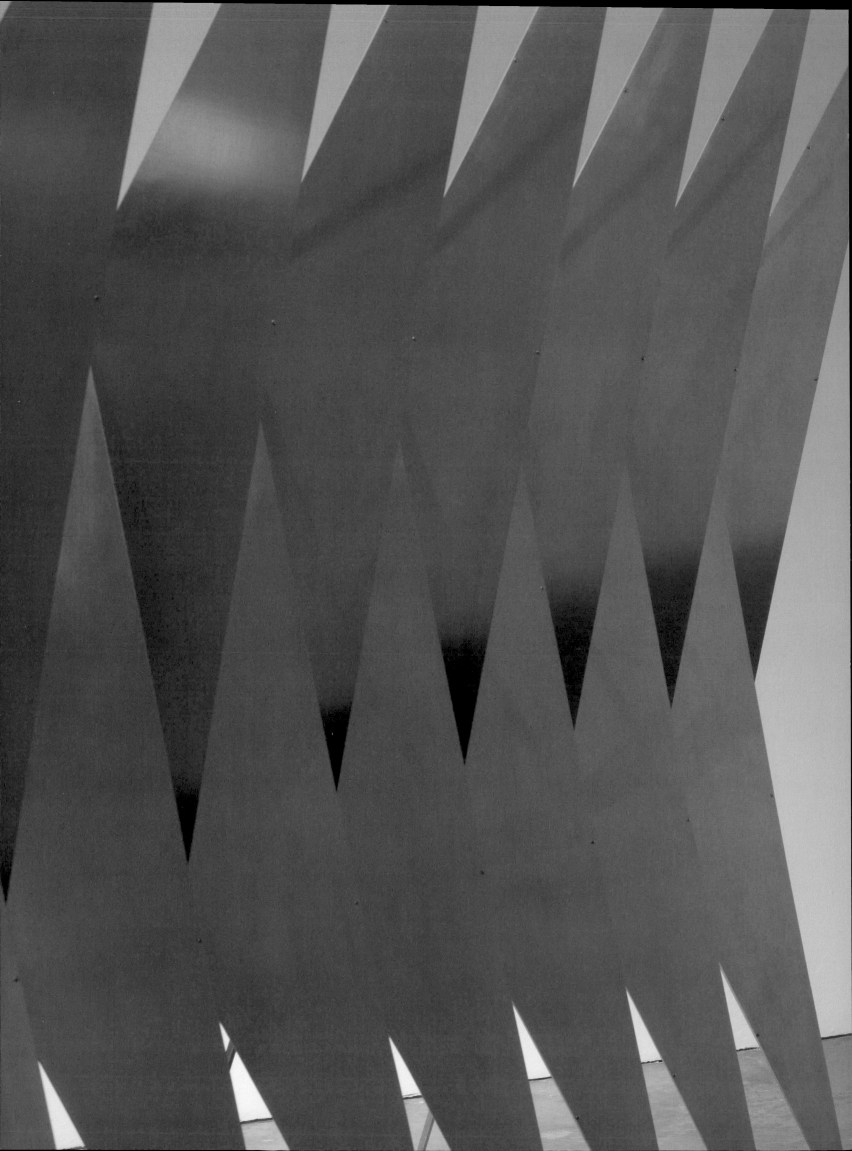

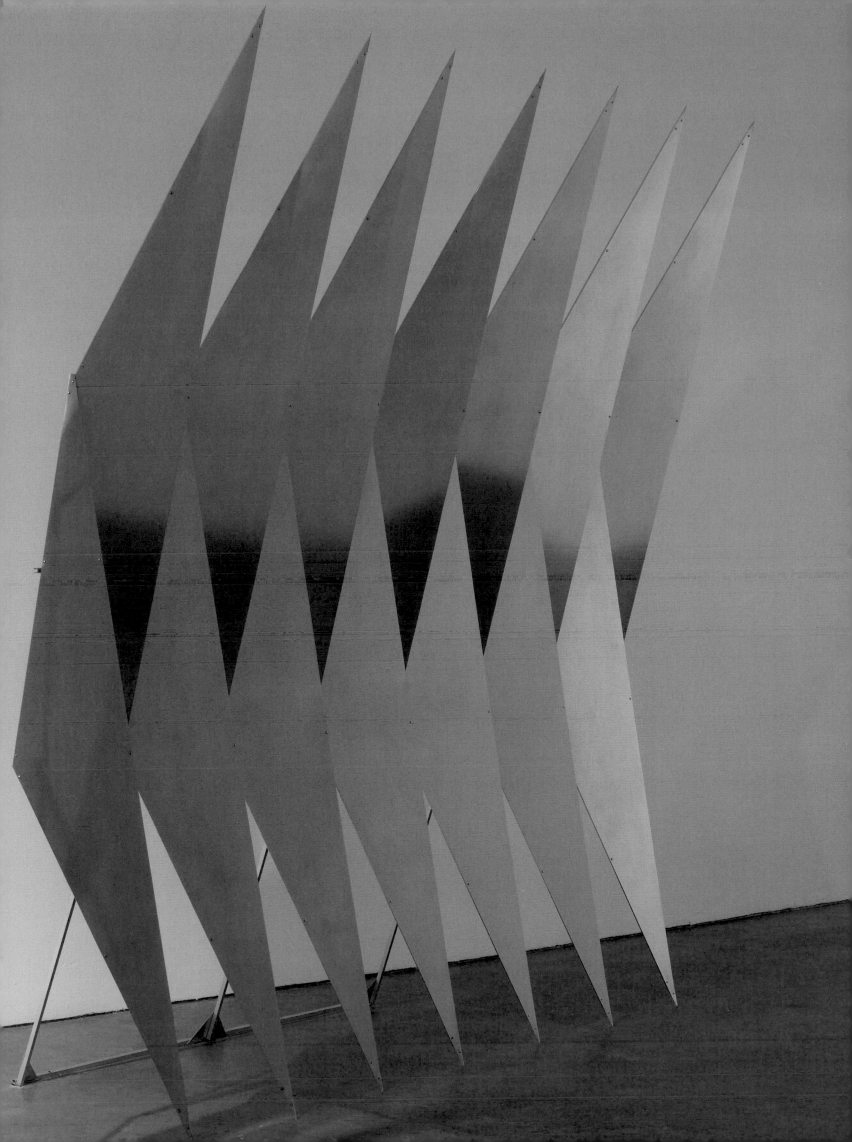

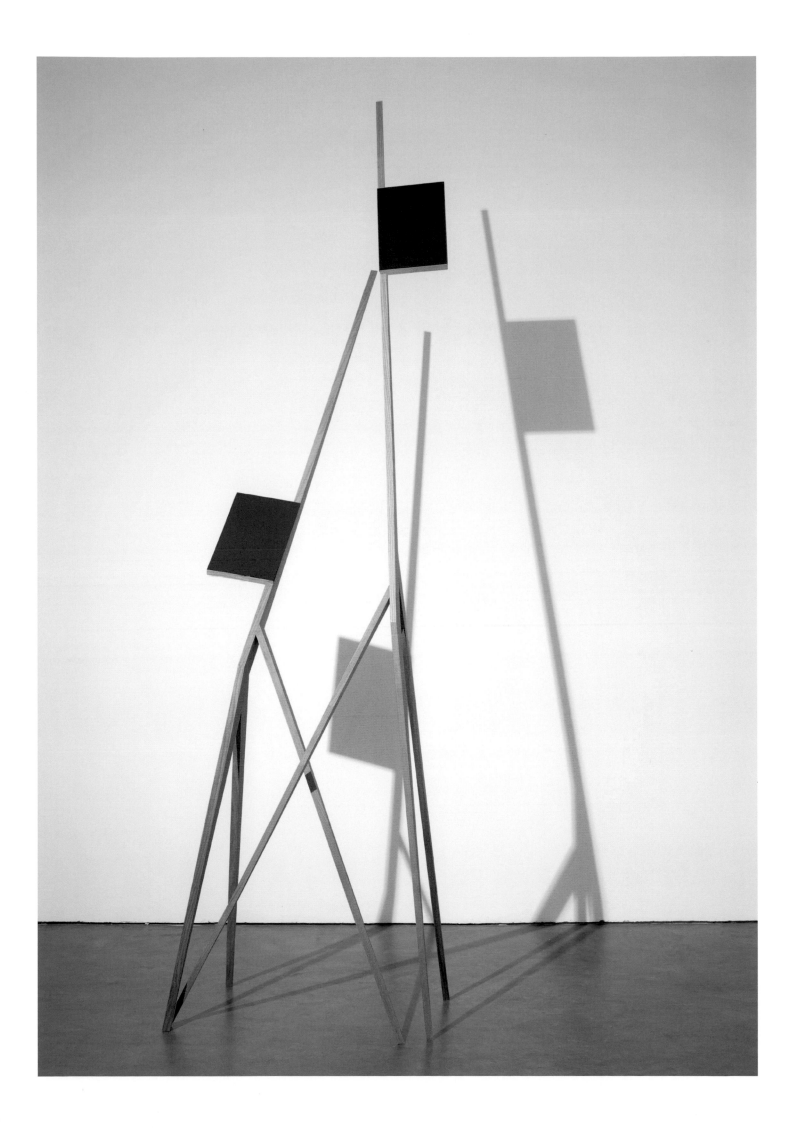

Robert Orchardson
Born Glasgow, Scotland, 1976

Solo Exhibitions

2009
New Model Army, Galerie Ben Kaufmann, Berlin

2007
Edge of the Superstructure, Galerie Ben Kaufmann, Berlin

2005
Perfect Vacuum, Wilkinson Gallery, London
Beyond, Monitor Gallery, Rome
Robert Orchardson, Economist Plaza, London

2004
Symmetriad, Galerie Ben Kaufmann, Munich

2002
News from Nowhere, The Changing Room Gallery, Stirling

Selected Group Exhibitions

2010
A Stranger's Window, Nottingham Castle Museum
A Cage Around the Sun, von Doering Contemporary,
Schwabisch Hall
The Associates, Dundee Contemporary Arts
7 x 2, Haus des Kindes / Henselmann Tower, Berlin
Plusdesign, Plusdesign Gallery, Milan

2008
The point of no return, Rubicon Gallery, Dublin
Let Me Show You Some Things, CCA, Glasgow
Masterpieces of the 21st Century, Galerie Ben Kaufmann, Berlin
Unfair Fair, 1:1projects, Rome
Ripe for revisiting on a daily basis, 52meters, London
Future50, Project Space, Leeds

2007
Robert Orchardson and Sarah Tripp, Generator Projects, Dundee
La Bomba IV, Rowley Kennerk Gallery, Chicago
All Hands on Deck, Galerie Ben Kaufmann, Munich
Last Show, Wilkinson Gallery, London
Artfutures 07, Bloomberg Space, London

2006
Robert Orchardson and Aleksandra Mir
International Project Space, Birmingham

2005
Liquid Crystal, Lothringer Dreizehn, Munich, Germany
Arte all' Arte, Castilo Linare, San Gimignano, Italy
Bloomberg New Contemporaries, Cornerhouse, Manchester;
LOT, Bristol; Barbican, London
Friday Night, All Saints Church, London

2004
Half of Life, Galerie Ben Kaufmann, Munich
Crystal Peaks, S1 Artspace, Sheffield

2003
Knights of the Holy Contact, Intermedia Gallery, Glasgow

2002
Earthly Paradise, Cooper Gallery, Dundee

2001
Beyond, Dundee Contemporary Arts, Dundee

2000
Forever, Dundee City Airport

1999
Tales of Ordinary Madness, Patriothall Gallery, Edinburgh
New Vision, Eye 2 Gallery, Edinburgh
Accelerated Learning, Duncan of Jordanstone College of Art
(DJCA), Dundee
Coming up for air, Cooper Gallery, Dundee

Robert Orchardson
Endless façade

Ikon Gallery, Birmingham
23 February – 25 April 2011

Contemporary Art Gallery, Vancouver
17 November 2011 – 8 January 2012

Curated by Nigel Prince
Assisted by Alexandra Lockett

ISBN 978-1-904864-68-4

Edited by Nigel Prince
Text by Matthew Rampley
Designed by James Langdon
Installation photography by Stuart Whipps
Printed by Die Keure, Belgium

All work courtesy of the artist and
Wilkinson Gallery, London
Galerie Ben Kaufmann, Berlin

Ikon Gallery
1 Oozells Square
Brindleyplace
Birmingham, B1 2HS
United Kingdom

Tel. +44 (0) 121 248 0708
Fax. +44 (0) 121 248 0709
www.ikon-gallery.co.uk
Registered charity no. 528892

Contemporary Art Gallery
555 Nelson Street
Vancouver
British Columbia, V6B 6R5
Canada

Tel. +1 604 681 2700
Fax. +1 604 683 2710
www.contemporaryartgallery.ca

Distributed by Cornerhouse Publications
70 Oxford Street, Manchester M1 5NH
Tel. +44 (0) 161 200 1503
Fax. +44 (0) 161 200 1504
publications@cornerhouse.org

Ikon acknowledges financial assistance from Arts Council
England and Birmingham City Council

The Contemporary Art Gallery is generously supported by
The Canada Council for the Arts, The Province of British
Columbia and the BC Arts Council, The City of Vancouver,
our members, donors and volunteers

IKON

Supported by
**ARTS COUNCIL
ENGLAND**

Birmingham City Council

CAG

CITY OF
VANCOUVER

Canada Council   Conseil des Arts
for the Arts   du Canada

**BRITISH
COLUMBIA**
The Best Place on Earth

BRITISH COLUMBIA
ARTS COUNCIL
An agency of the Province of British Columbia